SOMEWHERE IN
LA LA LAND

CHRISTINE AMELIA

Somewhere in La La Land
Copyright © 2024 by Christine Amelia.

All rights reserved. No part of this publication may be reproduced, distributed, or transmitted in any form or by any means, including photocopying, recording, or other electronic or mechanical methods, without the written consent of the publisher. The only exceptions are for brief quotations included in critical reviews and other noncommercial uses permitted by copyright law.

MILTON & HUGO L.L.C.
4407 Park Ave., Suite 5
Union City, NJ 07087, USA

Website: *www. miltonandhugo.com*
Hotline: *1- 888-778-0033*
Email: *info@miltonandhugo.com*

Ordering Information:
Quantity sales. Special discounts are granted to corporations, associations, and other organizations. For more information on these discounts, please reach out to the publisher using the contact information provided above.

Library of Congress Control Number: 2024912334
ISBN-13: 979-8-89285-175-6 [Paperback Edition]
979-8-89285-174-9 [Digital Edition]

Rev. date: 06/04/2024

TABLE OF CONTENTS

The Initial Heartbreak 1
The Withdrawals 25
The Final Heartbreak 43
The Other Side 59
Final Thoughts 67

ACKNOWLEDGEMENTS

For my title poem, Somewhere in la la land, I
drew inspiration from the film *La La Land*
directed by Damien Chazelle.
For the cover design, I was inspired by the
observatory scene in the film.
For the poem, The restaurant, I was inspired by
the song *Right Where You Left Me* by
Taylor Swift.
I would like to thank my friends and family for
their unwavering confidence in me.
None of this would be possible without them.

Damien Chazelle, Justin Hurwitz, Tim Davies, Steven Gizicki & Justin Hurwitz. (2016) "LA LA LAND" USA/Hong Kong.
Swift, T. (2020) Right Where You Left Me. On Evermore (deluxe version). Republic Records.

INTRODUCTION

Going through heartbreak is never easy. Losing someone you cared about so deeply is such a devastating feeling. Going through my first heartbreak I found solace in writing. This book was my healing journey. Writing this gave my feelings life in poem form. It was one of the most beautiful and rewarding two year experiences and I can not wait for you to read. I put my soul into this book; I hope you can find peace and comfort in my writings. Always remember, healing is not a linear journey. You may not even know what healed means for you yet. It is all about discovering yourself and who you are to your core. With this book I found myself.

The Initial Heartbreak

When going through my first breakup, I thought I was going to die.
I felt and wrote all of my emotions. Even
when it was uncomfortable at times.
This part faces the raw, scattered, and conflicting
emotions; of love, hate, and heartbreak

Falling in love

falling in love with you was the easiest thing to do
it was like breathing
from the minute you asked me to be your girlfriend
i wanted to tell you
falling in love with you was just so easy
i got wrapped up into falling in love with you
i fell in love with every part of you
i exposed myself to you and was completely vulnerable
and i let myself because i was in love with you
i got to experience the love that younger me never thought i
would experience
i wrote notes app essays about how much i loved you
i woke up next to you being grateful that you walked into my life
i was so in love with you
i still am
but you aren't in love with me anymore
and i continue to love you
falling in love with you was the easiest thing to do
it was like breathing
falling out of love with you
is drowning me
so instead of drowning and gasping for air
i continue to breathe it in
i chose to love you because i would rather love you than drown
and have to relearn how to breathe a
different type of air

Man's best friend

sitting, begging, waiting for you
i want to be loved like a person, not a dog

Somewhere in la la land

you have the best imagination when you're a little kid
you can make friends
create worlds
you can do anything in your mind
people often refer to this as day dreaming
going off on an adventure
somewhere in la la land
where creativity blooms
flowers sing
an escape from the cold truth
you're not mine anymore.
you're still with me in la la land
i can see now why it's your favorite movie.

Too

i always thought that saying too after i love you was odd
i love you too
it feels like when you are saying it you are only doing it out of obligation
now when i look through our old texts and remember how i told you this
i wonder if sometimes you wished you added the "too"

Darling

oh my darling
it was never you
it was never your fault
and i know you keep blaming yourself and keep reliving everything you could've done different
darling
it was never you
you are the person who pours their soul into another even if it means you lose yourself in the process
you grace this earth with so much love that it pours out of you everywhere you go
darling
it was never you
you would've moved mountains for him
you would've taken his pain and bore it along with all of the pain you're experiencing
darling
it was never you
the love you gave you can not take back but do not regret it because even if you can't remember the feeling right now
remember that he loved you
darling
it was never you
he would've moved mountains for you
he would've taken your pain and bore it along with all of the pain he was experiencing
so darling remember
it was never you
the universe knew that you needed each other
and now you must trust that it will bring you back together because
darling
it was never you

Fireball

the same melancholy feeling dreads over me everyday
maybe i need to start drinking whiskey like we used too

You who will <u>always</u> be named

every person i will ever love
from the moment we met onwards
will know your name
know the place you have in my life
the hold you have on me
how your grasp on me seems to only grow tighter
i can't get you out
you are coursing through my veins
and I am struggling to come to terms
with the fact that I will have to
live the rest of my life like this

Gifts

it's my love language
giving gifts to people
letting them know that i'm thinking about them
that i care about them and bought them a gift to show it
almost prove my love for that person
but you were my gift
yes of course we gave each other things
but YOU were my gift
everything was just so easy
it just felt so natural
like it was supposed to be the two of us
and i know that you'll fall in love again
i hope you know that no one will ever love you the same way i did
yes you will be loved
you will always be loved
but not in the same way i still do

Hitting restart

yesterday you said you didn't want this to be the end
so i restarted my clock
i reset everything going on in my head telling me to get over you
it was so simple to forget
everything
every negative feeling i had towards you
all of the resentment
the slivers of hatred forming
the piles of disappointment
formed from false promises
everything
all for you
because deep down i never stopped loving you
i never fell out of love
so i restarted my clock
and now i'll wait until we begin again

Interlinked

our souls are intertwined
they were destined to meet
in every lifetime
in every universe
every century
our cells were meant to meet
and our souls needed to touch
because no matter how far away we run from it
we both know it's true
that no matter what i do i will always be in love with you

The gloat

it was like i was in a movie
the girl dating her celebrity crush
i was starstruck
the small town girl
with the singer
who would go on to write love songs about her
even when we weren't in love anymore
writing songs about how we shared
the greatest love of all time
and you'll go off and get famous
become a real star
but i'm not your muse anymore
so i can't keep listening to your music
pretending you are still in love with me

Star crossed lovers

i believe that we were star crossed lovers
lovers who were only meant for a short period of time
lovers who could not end up together
we were the love story that we'd tell our children about
we were the tale of the greatest love story
where we felt so alive
the young love bloomed into something we couldn't have ever imagined
but we were also the story that we would tell during our kids first heartbreak
because our future kids wouldn't be the kids we had together
we would tell them the story of how things aren't always meant to be
that sometimes no matter how much you love someone
they're only meant to be in your life temporarily
because sometimes the greatest love story
is also your greatest heartache

Empty bed sheets

i sleep in your bedsheets
every night i go to bed warm
underneath your covers and laying my head on your pillow
you left your bedsheets
but i still sleep with them every night
i pull them over me to protect me from the cold
i lay in them before i go to work
when my friends come over they sit on my bed
they tell me how comfy the blankets are and ask where i got them from
the look i get every time i tell someone they're yours is the same
the sadness
the pity
shines right through their sorrowful gaze
because i still sleep in your bed sheets
but the comfort of having them wrapped around me every night
almost makes the bed feel less empty
almost brings me back to when you were the one who wrapped me up tight
but until that can happen again
i sleep in your bed sheets every night

False rings

you told me your friends bet that you would get married first and
that it would be to me
i never want to let another person know me the way you did

Madness

the ascent into madness is slow
it starts by things feeling a little off
and then you become anxious about everything
everything
the shadows in the corners of your room
the noise that the fan makes
the way that you look
everything
and then all of the sudden it collapses
everything
it caves in all around you
the madness consumes you
you and everything you do
every movement
every decision
every small thought that runs through your brain
everything
but the scariest thing about madness
is you can truly never know when it began
or when it will end

Broken systems

it was never discussed
but it was always in place
this system of risk and reward
if i did the right things
and i said the right words
i would have a loving caring boyfriend
but if i did too much
if i asked to go out
if i said the wrong thing at the wrong time
it was like you were a completely different person
who hated me
who hated anything i tried to do to save us
and at the end of the day you always ran
because that's how the system was built
when times got hard
you ran
i stayed
you will keep running for the rest of your life
while i stay here trying to repair the system

It's killing me

the obsession is what kills you
knowing that they're happy
enjoying their life
living without you
and that it's okay to them
you can't even get out of bed
but they are out there
doing everything you always talked about
all you can do is scroll away
checking their social medias
drafting texts
crying until you can't breathe
but they are out there
breathing fresh air
experiencing life
and no matter what you do you can't pull yourself out of this hole
so you just observe through a screen
wishing that things were different
wishing that your absence kills them as much as theirs kills you

Absent questions

how can my absence not bother you?
how are you not physically sick by the fact that we are not together?
how are you living your life completely fine as if none of this is even phasing you?
was i really that easy to get over?
did you really love me?
or was that another one of your lies

The waiting game

i've been known to be competitive when it comes to board games
screaming
fighting
flipping the board
but never to be the person who plays emotional ones
i like to think i am honest with my emotions
i don't like to play around with other people's feelings
but the one game i've mastered
the waiting one
because i would wait for you
you are the only person i want to walk toward
the only person i would ever play a game like this with
because to me you are worth waiting for

My purple flame sweater

i want to set it on fire
i want to know that no one will ever wear it again
i can't donate it because i don't want someone else to wear my sweater
but i can't get rid of it
i can't get rid of you
i want to set it on fire and watch as the threads slowly burn into ash
one by one
the fire pattern on the sweater would be engulfed in real flames
i want to watch as the memories burn along with it
except i don't
because i never want to forget you
or any of the memories we made together
so instead i will just burn the sweater
my purple sweater
and as i set it on fire
know that my heart still burns for you

A letter to my lover

my love
you are the most perfect person in the world
you second guess yourself and don't give yourself enough credit
you make my days infinitely better
you make it so that forever doesn't seem sufficient
you are my perfect person
even if you aren't perfect
you're perfect to me
and that's all that matters really
i am so infatuated by your existence
and how you pour yourself into other people
how caring you are to the ones you love
how much you care and want to protect me from every evil this world has to offer
i am so endlessly in love with you
and forever proud of the person you are and the person you're going to become
i hope in another universe i get to tell you all of these things
and remind you constantly how much i love you
because i do
i love you
forever and ever and always
but until we meet again my love
i'll just have to write this message
and hope that someday i can show you

The Withdrawals

When going through my breakup, I found that months
would go by but I would still have the itch to
reach out. I felt like I needed to talk to him, break
the no contact. This part faces the emotions of
wanting to talk but knowing you can't; and all
of the emotions that surround that.

Scabs

no contact.
no texting.
no calling.
not sending a pigeon with a message attached to its foot.
nothing.
but sometimes you want to break it
you want to reach out
you want to check in and see how they're doing
you want to tell them how much you miss them and how you want them back in your life
my mother told me that breaking no contact was like my one bad habit
picking scabs
because every time you pick a scab
it gets closer to scarring
and once it's scarred you can't undo it
she told me how if i ever wanted things to work out the way they should i should stop picking the scab
she told me how if i kept reaching out begging for a response from you it would permanently scar
and once the scar forms
there's no turning back

The end of summer

it's the end of summer
well almost
the end of July is a reminder that school is starting soon
and once school starts it'll be September
and after September it'll be October
and October is when i met you
that's when everything changed
October is when i saw myself falling in love
after all of the terrible things to happen to me
October is when i saw the light at the end of the tunnel
October turned to November
and November is when we started dating
November is when we drunkenly said i love you for the first time
November is when i decided you were my person
November is when i decided that you were the person i wanted to spend the rest of my life with
so how is it the end of the summer?
how can it almost be October
where October leads to November
which will eventually turn into June
and June is when you left
how can it be the end of the summer?
where i'll have to experience all of these months again but without you

Love/addiction

it affects the same chemicals in your brain
codependency and meth
i am actually addicted to you
not figuratively
or poetically
but quite literally addicted to you
and going sober
quitting you cold turkey would mean that i could never do it again
i could never talk to you again
and i don't think i would like to ever live in a world where we aren't talking
so i don't think i can go no contact
because I don't think i can quit you just yet

Cravings

smoking isn't healthy but it's an escape
it makes time move slower
it makes shows funnier than they really are
it makes you crave food
it alters your mindset so you perceive everything differently even if you don't realize it
smoking makes me remember and forget
i forget that you left
i remember how we used to smoke in the cave on the side of the highway
i smoke and instead of craving food
all i crave is you
i crave your presence
to hear you laugh at one of my stupid jokes
to feel our bodies touch as we lay in bed
to hold your hand as you drive
to scream old Justin Bieber while our friends are in the backseat
i crave you
all of the time
but when i'm high it is my only thought
if i'm not trying to forget you
and failing to do so
i'm still thinking about you
because when i'm high
all i think about is you

Drunk words/sober thoughts

i think there's something so poetic about drunk poetry
how easy it is to express everything
in the most eloquent manner while still being gutting
and to pour my soul into something so small
so simple
yet so profound
how words strung together can spark such intense emotions
that it needs to be spilled out into a poem
my drunk words are my sober thoughts
and my drunk thoughts are my sober ones amplified
so instead of sending the drunk text
i'll sit with my thoughts and write

Chapped

you know that feeling when your lips are chapped
and no matter how much lip balm you use
or the amount of times that you lick your lips
you always end up just biting the skin off
afterwards you feel so much better
until they start bleeding
and swelling
just to become chapped all over again
then you are reminded why you don't bite your lips

Vortex

it's like a pit in your stomach
not like normal stomach aches
but as if there is a black hole forming inside of you
sucking you in
into the darkness
the all consuming pit
it forms whenever i think about you
think about the time we've shared
the memories we have
i get sucked back in into the sadness that i've pushed away for so long
forced to face the feelings
accept the fate we have
wish for days on end that it can be different
but you don't feel the same way

Your obituary

i think my life was easier
when i lived my life as if you were dead

The restaurant

the menu's changed since i was last there
i heard from the reviews that there's always the prettiest flowers on display now.
i don't remember ever seeing flowers from our booth
i heard that you sit at the bar now
we always sat in the corner so we could sit next to each other and both be comfortable
i pass it by sometimes and catch myself looking in
seeing the corner untouched and just the way i left it
i'm not so sure i ever did though
i've brought new people to the restaurant
but unlike you i still sit in the corner booth
and i have it in my head that if i stay there they'll have to be like you
they have to fit your expectations
fit the standard you left me with
so maybe i'm still at the restaurant
and the menu changed
and i'll still introduce people to your spot
in the corner booth
order the same food
tell the same stories
still have the expectation that i can make the same memories
until the day you ask if you could take a seat
and i'll get to tell you that i've been keeping it warm for you

A dying flame

i've taken so many pictures since it ended
not just of myself but everything around me
i've found beauty in the world the surrounds me and captured it
into photos
but i've also taken pictures with me in it
and they look good
but there's something off
you used to tell me that my eyes took you to outer space
that there was a light in my eyes
and i never noticed it
until i've looked at the pictures i've taken since you've left
and i can't seem to find the light
the light in my eyes died the day you left
there was no more sparkle
no more hope
just lifeless brown eyes

Missing you

i miss you
do you know how embarrassing that is to admit?
that i miss you
that i would do anything just to hear your voice
that if you showed up at my door that i would just let you in
without question
it's so humiliating
i miss you
so similar to the three words i used to tell you
i loved you with every fiber in my being
it was like pieces of you ran through my veins
i was addicted to you
i just couldn't get enough
i loved you more than anything in this world including myself
and here i am
still in love with you
still waiting for you
because i miss you
and i really want you to come home soon

Take it back

it should have never ended like this
i know in my heart that this is not the end of our story
i don't want this to be the end
i miss you
i know you miss me too
so if you can't move on
and you want to call
i would love to pick up the phone
and restart
because this shouldn't be the end of us
it was only the beginning of our story

Last

i want it to be you
i still want it to be you in the end
even though you're long gone
and you've probably already moved on
i told you we were a type of love to last
and i mean that
to this day i mean that
you are my person
the love of my life
i really hope we're the type of love to come back

Forever

i told you i'd love you forever
forever and ever and always
i didn't know then that our forever would fall apart
i didn't know that i'd love you forever but i wouldn't get that
forever with you
that i'd be so in love with you that months later
i'd be here
in love with you
i never wanted to imagine this happening
let alone live through it
our forever fell apart
i should've known that this would happen
so now i'll spend forever
loving you
until forever stops
and hopefully between then and now
we can restart

The fifteenth

i wonder if you saw today's date
did you notice it was the fifteenth?
did you remember that today would've been our anniversary
or did you look at today and just think of it as any other day
do you ever think about me
do i cross your mind at all?
do you ever wonder what i'm doing?
i still think about you sometimes
and it hurts
physically
to even think about you with her
to think that you tell her all of the things you used to say to me
kills me
but soon i'll be saying new things
to a new person
and i won't think about you
but todays the fifteenth
and i remembered
did you?

The Final Heartbreak

The ex cycle. Where you let them back in until you hate them. I fell victim to the ex cycle and let him back in, multiple times. Spoiler alert: he didn't change, they never do. This part faces the emotions of realizing it is truly over.

What if he isn't you?

i really wish i could hate you for everything you put me through
i wish that i could say that i hated you and meant it
but i still love you
i'll always love you
i'll always miss the way you looked at me
and the way you said my name
the feeling of being in your arms
i'll always love you because you are my first love
i thought you'd be my only love
the person i'd spend the rest of my life with
i know that will never happen now
but the thought of being in love with anyone other than you
makes me sick
what if he isn't you?
what if he won't have a frosting fight in the kitchen
what if he doesn't hold my hand when he drives
or refuses to sing with me in the car
or worse
what if he doesn't love me as much as you did?
i loved you more than i could ever put into words
i'll always love you
i wish you loved me like you said you always would

Mean

you're being mean
you realized that i was moving on and that i stopped putting in the effort
so now you decide you're ready
that you want to watch our show together
after you made me watch it alone
you tell me to have fun knowing that i'm going to a party
you tell me that you want to get back together
but why now
why was our last conversation longer than our breakup
why did you act like you cared
we both know you don't
you're giving me false hope that you're going to come back
you're being mean
if you ever loved me you wouldn't be doing this
you wouldn't have treated me so poorly just to change your mind
you wouldn't keep me on a leash and tug me back when i go too far
you would just let me go completely
if you ever loved me you would've told me from the beginning
that you always had intentions of
coming back
you would've told me so that i wouldn't have nearly killed myself trying to move on from this
and then drag me back in after i start experiencing life again
you're being mean
and i don't know if i want to go back

Did you know?

did you know i loved you?
with everything in me and more
i loved you
and you walked away from me
and us
and all the plans we made
and i'll always hate you for ruining my birthday
and i'll always love you for being there for me when i needed you
but now i have to stop
i have to let you go
you have to let me go
because i have the opportunity to be happy
and to love someone
and to be everything to someone again
so know that i loved you
with everything in me and more
and know that i want nothing more than for you to be happy
but i have to be happy too

274 days

it's been 274 days since the last time i wrote for you
wanted to hear your voice
i'm supposed to be happy now
it's been 380 days since we broke up
i'm with someone new now too
you said he was cool
but i always thought you were the coolest person i had ever met
and you're right he is
but you asked me to lunch
and make my heart lunge out of my chest when i see your name on my phone
sometimes i swear you live in my walls and can hear my every thought
that's why you do the things that you do
you just know
i miss knowing you
it's been 274 days since the last time i wrote for you
and i've had so many things i've wanted to say
but i think the things i've wanted to say the most would be
i'm proud of you
i miss you
and oh how i love you
and how no matter how hard i try i don't think i could ever stop

V.I.P. status

i put in the rsvp
i saved you a seat
i got the tickets already booked
but the chair remains empty
there is no one to fill the seat
the metal stays cold
i put on the performance of a lifetime
i looked through the crowds
trying to find you
see if you finally showed up for me
and the sign was still there
"Very Important Person"
but you weren't
you didn't show up
you never show up
i have to stop believing you will
clearly you never believed in me
or
i am just not as important to you
as you are to me

Quitting

you're still the same
in my head i have this version of you
where you have matured
learned how to prioritize yourself
and the people you love
i used to be a person you loved
once upon a time i was the love of your life
this version i have of you in my head still thinks i am the love of your life
he makes promises and actually keeps them
it's this crazy concept
not that you would know
you're still the same
i thought i liked that
that you were still you
but the person i am now knows better
so i'll wait until you are the version i have of you in my head

Who are you?

you constantly disappoint me
you make it so hard to remember that you were the man i once loved
i just can't believe how cold you've gotten
how you could continue to run away from every problem in your life
how you ran away from us
how selfish you are
i can't believe i ever loved you
or that i ever trusted you
or that i ever saw a future with the you
the person you are now is not the person i fell in love with
and i mean that in the most
gut wrenching
heartbreaking
disappointed
way

I was in love with you

it's crazy isn't it
the things it does to you
it makes you crazy
i went crazy
being in love with you drove me insane
thinking that i could just give you every piece of me
that i could let you be the mastermind behind my every move
every thought
that if i let you be in control you'd never leave
that you'd love me too
but we were never in love
not really
i loved you with everything i had in me
and you loved that i loved you
and the power that came with that
and so now i'm sitting here
reflecting on our "love story"
and wondering if that's the only type of love in the cards for me
that if all i'm ever going to be seen as is the girl you could suck the life out of
and use until you're bored
or find someone new
or decide that it's just not worth it
love is crazy
complicated
confusing
and i don't think i'll ever understand it
because you permanently tainted love for me

Hostage

i felt trapped
trapped by my anxiety
trapped by my emotions
and i didn't know how to escape
the prison walls were so dark i couldn't tell what was trapping me
when you left i finally got to see what was holding me hostage
my anxiety started waving goodbye to me as if i was an old friend
as the light burst through the prison doors
while i was leaving i turned back and saw all of the pain that i was holding onto
how i was riddled with so much fear that you would leave that i became trapped
i was in a cell where all i could worry about was you
worry about every word i said to you
worried about how one day you would give up on me
worried that i wasn't good enough for you
how you deserved better
but you never deserved to know me
the prison i was once held hostage in set me free
free to learn how to see the world
without worrying about you
and if we cross paths again
i will never be yours to hold hostage

I hate you

three words
eight letters
but not the ones you would expect
i hate you
i hate the way you treat me like i'm nothing
and how you left me all broken and wrecked
i hate the way it's so easy for you to ignore me
how i used to worship the ground you walked on
but now i realize you never deserved my respect

The final heartbreak

everyone always tells you after a breakup how the initial
heartbreak is the worst
but its not
what about when you find out he moved on right after you
broke up
the feeling that you can't breathe
as you are wailing on the floor
begging for help to stand
or the feeling of trying to get into a new relationship
trying to love the wrong person
knowing that you are meant to be with someone else
what about when you find out that he's still in love with you
after all this time
so you call him
tell him everything you've always dreamed of
but then he gets into a new relationship
you become single
all you want to do is reach out
just one more call
but you can't
what about when almost two years since he initially broke your
heart
when he was supposed to be changed
a better man
so you let him back in
and he continues to make empty promises
continues to hurt you
two years later
two years since the initial heartbreak
i don't know but i think this is worse

The come down

it was a beautiful trip
the visuals
the performance we put on during the come up
we were perfect
to everyone around us we were this spectacle of a couple
the peak of our time together
the adventures we went on
the things that we did
it was like it was out of a movie
i needed to know how to keep this going
i never wanted it to end
than there was a pause
it felt like a glitch in time
the come down was sudden
all of the lights went dark
there was no more adventure
it was no longer perfect
i was able to see it all from a different perspective
as i watched back and reflected i realized it was never perfect
we were never perfect
than the trip was over
you were gone
the visuals dissipated
life returned to almost the same
except now you are gone
and i am happy about it

Over it

i never thought i'd see the day where i gave up on you
i don't think it happened as instantaneous as i'd like
i think it started over the days without any response from you
the nights i spent wallowing in my pain
constantly looking at my phone desperately waiting for a text from you
torturing myself over what i could've done to deserve this treatment from you
and then finally hit after you sent that half assed apology for not answering me when i needed you most
that i just looked at your name in my phone
and felt absolutely nothing.

The Other Side

The first thing most people told me when
going through my breakup was,
"that life will be so much better now that
you're on the other side of it".
I felt that I would never make it to the other side.
I didn't believe the other side was real.
This part faces the emotions of realizing that you've made it.

Someone new

i wonder how you'd feel if you knew i met someone
someone that isn't you
i wonder if your skin would crawl knowing i was laying in bed
with him
if you saw the way i looked at him how i used to look at you
if you could feel how fast my heart was beating
or how excited i was to go see him
i had taken an extra long time to do my makeup
do you think he noticed?
i know you would have
i wonder if you saw how much i was smiling
if you'd even realize that this was the first time i'd smiled like that
since you've left
but it doesn't matter now
just knowing that i could look at someone with such adoration the
same as i did you
means that i know i can move on from you
onto someone new

What is moving on?

one day i woke up and i was happy
i was happy that i woke up
i was happy that i was alive and got to experience that day
i wasn't thinking about how my heart felt like i shredded it
after ripping it into a thousand pieces
i wasn't thinking about how much i missed you
i wasn't thinking about you at all
suddenly it was noon
i went out and i got a compliment on my bracelet
the one that i have that matches with you
i laughed and said thanks
then continued on my day
instead of thinking about how angry i was that this was over
after everything we went through
i thought about how happy i was the day we got the bracelets
i thought about you as if you were a distant memory
and suddenly i'm falling asleep
and instead of dreaming that night about how you'll suddenly
decide to show up
give us another chance
i went to bed smiling knowing that i had the opportunity to love you
even if it wasn't for a long period of time

The love of my life.

there are so many words that i could write
i could write about how much i'm still in love with you
how i know it will never work out
how it will never be the same as before
or how much i hate you
for still being the
same
disappointing
excuse of a man
how much i hate myself for letting you back in
but instead i think i'll find something new to write about
because there is only so many things that can be said about a
person
and i am done writing about you.

The final realization

this journey of self love and hatred
finding myself
has finally come to a close
this chapter of my life
has built up to this moment
the culminating point of it all
my final realization
no matter how much i love you
it will never be enough
AND THAT IS OKAY
because you never deserved to know me in the first place

The other side

i think i've finally made it
i've thought that i made it here before
it looks much different now
now when i look towards my future i don't see you in it
at all
there is no room for you anymore
this other side that everyone talks about
actually looks like there can be good
like i went through it all for something
for some greater purpose
i finally made it here
and that's the first step

Final Thoughts

I love writing. It's my creative outlet. Poetry lets me express my emotions and turn them into something beautiful. My sophomore year high school teacher introduced me into the world of poetry. He taught me that anyone could write poetry, even me. I have decided to leave the last pages of my first book blank. Everyone deserves the opportunity and the space to find their own voice. Whether you are still going through the initial heartbreak, the withdrawals, the final heartbreak, the other side, or anywhere in between; I invite you to write about your feelings and your journey through heartbreak. It can be cathartic writing art.